Pebble® Plus

Under the Sea

Sea Turtles

by Carol K. Lindeen

Consulting Editor: Gail Saunders-Smith, PhD

Consultant: Jody Rake, Member
Southwest Marine/Aquatic Educator's Association

Capstone press

Mankato, Minnesota

Pebble Plus is published by Capstone Press,
151 Good Counsel Drive, P.O. Box 669, Mankato, Minnesota 56002.
www.capstonepub.com

Library of Congress Cataloging-in-Publication Data
Lindeen, Carol K., 1976–
   Sea turtles / by Carol K. Lindeen.
   p. cm.—(Pebble Plus: Under the sea)
   Includes bibliographical references (p. 23) and index.
   ISBN 978-0-7368-2601-3 (hardcover)
   ISBN 978-0-7368-5113-8 (softcover pbk.)
   ISBN 978-1-4296-5067-0 (saddle-stitched)
   1. Sea turtles—Juvenile literature. [1. Sea turtles. 2. Turtles.] I. Title. II. Series.
QL666.C536L56 2005
597.92′8—dc22   2003025611

Summary: Simple text and photographs present the lives of sea turtles.

Editorial Credits
Martha E. H. Rustad, editor; Juliette Peters, designer; Kelly Garvin, photo researcher;
   Karen Hieb, product planning editor

Photo Credits
DigitalVision/Stephen Frink, 1
Michael Patrick O'Neill, 8–9
Minden Pictures/Birgitte Willms, cover; Mike Parry, 16–17, 18–19
PhotoDisc Inc., back cover
Seapics.com/David B. Fleetham, 4–5, 20–21; Doug Perrine, 6–7, 10–11; James D. Watt, 12–13, 14–15

Note to Parents and Teachers

The Under the Sea series supports national science standards related to the diversity
and unity of life. This book describes and illustrates sea turtles. The images support
early readers in understanding the text. The repetition of words and phrases helps early
readers learn new words. This book also introduces early readers to subject-specific
vocabulary words, which are defined in the Glossary section. Early readers may need
assistance to read some words and to use the Table of Contents, Glossary, Read More,
Internet Sites, and Index/Word List sections of the book.

Word Count: 118
Early-Intervention Level: 14

Printed in China
5896/5888/5887   082010

Table of Contents

Sea Turtles

What are sea turtles?

Sea turtles are reptiles.

Sea turtles poke their beaks
out of the water to breathe.

Sea turtles swim and crawl
with their flippers. Hard
shells protect the soft bodies
of sea turtles.

Migrating

Some sea turtles migrate.
They swim far to find
food and mates.

Sea turtles find currents of
warm water. The currents
help sea turtles swim
long distances quickly.

Female sea turtles crawl
on beaches. They dig
holes and lay their eggs.

Young sea turtles hatch on beaches. They hurry to the sea to find safety.

Under the Sea

Sea turtles swim
under the sea.

Index/Word List

Under the Sea

Titles in this set:

Crabs
Clown Fish
Dolphins
Sea Stars
Sea Turtles
Sharks
Whales

Sea turtles have hard shells and beaks. They migrate through the ocean, and crawl on land to lay their eggs. Learn about the lives of sea turtles under the sea.

Young readers will eagerly plunge into these dazzling books full of large, colorful underwater photography. Simple text makes it fun to read and learn all about these creatures and their amazing lives.

RL: 1   IL: PreK-2

Capstone Press
a capstone imprint

www.capstonepub.com

ISBN 978-1-4296-5067-0

90000

9 781429 650670